KETANJI BROWN JACKSON

Making a Difference as a Supreme Court Justice

By Katie Kawa

KidHaven
PUBLISHING

People Who Make a Difference

Published in 2025 by
KidHaven Publishing, an Imprint of Greenhaven Publishing, LLC
2544 Clinton St.
Buffalo, NY 14224

Designer: Deanna Lepovich
Editor: Katie Kawa

Photo credits: Cover American Photo Archive/Alamy Stock Photo; pp. 5 (main), 17 US Supreme Court/Alamy Stock Photo; p. 5 (inset) Rena Schild/Shutterstock.com; pp. 7, 9 Sipa USA/Alamy Stock Photo; p. 11 MediaPunch Inc/Alamy Stock Photo; p. 13 Xinhua/Alamy Stock Photo; p. 15 Abaca Press/Alamy Stock Photo; p. 18 Supreme Court of the United States - Roberts Court 2022/Wikimedia Commons; p. 21 T.Sumaetho/Shutterstock.com.

Cataloging-in-Publication Data

Names: Kawa, Katie.
Title: Ketanji Brown Jackson / Katie Kawa.
Description: Buffalo, NY : KidHaven Publishing, 2025. | Series: Points of view | Includes glossary and index.
Identifiers: ISBN 9781534548732 (pbk.) | ISBN 9781534548749 (library bound) | ISBN 9781534548756 (ebook)
Subjects: LCSH: Jackson, Ketanji Brown, 1970–Juvenile literature. | United States. Supreme Court–Juvenile literature. | Judges–United States.–Juvenile literature.
Classification: LCC KF8745.J25 K38 2025 | DDC 347.73'2634 B–dc23

Printed in the United States of America

CONTENTS

MAKING HISTORY

The Supreme Court is the highest court in the United States. The judges who serve on that court are called justices, and they have the power to make a big difference in the lives of the American people. Decisions made by Supreme Court justices have changed American history and continue to **affect** Americans today.

On June 30, 2022, Ketanji Brown Jackson joined the small group of Americans who've served on this court, becoming the first Black woman to do so. How did a young girl from Miami, Florida, grow up to make history? Keep reading to find out!

In Her Words

"I might be the first, but I don't want to be the last."

— Interview with the *Washington Post* from May 2022

Ketanji Brown Jackson is shown above taking an oath—a formal promise—before becoming a Supreme Court justice. All Supreme Court justices take oaths to do their job fairly and support the U.S. Constitution—the set of laws that created the U.S. government.

LEARNING FROM HER PARENTS

Ketanji's story began in Washington, D.C., long before she began working there. She was born there on September 14, 1970. Not long after, though, her family moved to Miami, which is where she spent her childhood. Her parents—Johnny and Ellery—were public school teachers who later became school officials.

Johnny and Ellery taught their children—Ketanji and her younger brother Ketajh—that knowledge is power. This included knowledge of Black history. They wanted their children to know about the Black men and women who worked hard so their **generation** could have a better life.

In Her Words

"[My parents] gave me an African name, and … set out to ensure [make sure] that I could do anything I wanted to do … They wanted most of all to prepare me for what they fervently [strongly] believed would be a great … future."

— Speech given in Alabama on September 15, 2023

Ketanji's brother and parents are shown here watching her answer questions before she became a Supreme Court justice. Ketanji has said that her father **inspired** her to become a lawyer. She would watch him study for law school while she colored in her coloring books as a little kid!

MOST LIKELY TO SUCCEED

Ketanji did well in school, and she was a good leader. She was elected class president at Miami Palmetto Senior High School and was voted "most likely to succeed" by her classmates.

Ketanji was involved in speech and **debate** in high school. She took part in **competitions** and won! Ketanji wanted to go to Harvard University in Massachusetts after high school. However, her **guidance counselor** told her not to dream that big. It was a good thing she didn't listen! Ketanji began studying at Harvard in 1988, right after graduating, or finishing, high school.

In Her Words

"It's not just what you say that leaves an impact ... It's also how you say it."

— Speech given to graduates of Boston University Law School in May 2023

Ketanji met Patrick Graves Jackson (shown here) at Harvard. They got married in 1996, and they have two daughters. Talia was born in 2000, and Leila was born in 2004.

BECOMING A LAWYER

Ketanji stayed busy at Harvard. She took acting classes and enjoyed being on stage. She also used her voice to call attention to problems at Harvard that were affecting Black students and teachers.

In 1992, she graduated from Harvard. She then worked for *TIME* magazine before returning to Harvard for law school. She finished law school in 1996 and began working as a lawyer. She worked in private practice and also as a law clerk for **federal** judges. Law clerks help lawyers and judges by researching, or gathering facts, and writing opinions, which formally explain a ruling made by a judge.

In Her Words

"I will note that these are subjects about which I care deeply. I have **dedicated** my career [work] to public service because I love this country and … the rights that make us free."

— Speech given on April 8, 2022

Ketanji was an editor of the *Harvard Law Review* while she was in law school. This is a collection of articles dealing with legal issues. Other famous Americans have also been editors of the *Harvard Law Review*, including John G. Roberts Jr., who's the current chief justice of the Supreme Court. He's shown here with Ketanji.

HELPING OTHERS

Ketanji has used her skills as a lawyer to help people in different ways. In 2003, she joined a group called the U.S. **Sentencing** Commission. Its job is to make sure federal sentencing rules are fair and just. She left that job in 2005 but returned to the commission in 2010 as one of its leaders.

From 2005 to 2007, Ketanji worked as a federal public defender in Washington, D.C. This kind of lawyer defends people who are **accused** of a crime but can't afford to pay for their own lawyer.

In Her Words

"You do not need to become someone you are not. You do you. Lean into your personal strengths and use them to get you where you want to go."

— Speech given to graduates of American University Washington College of Law in May 2023

Ketanji became the first former federal public defender to serve on the Supreme Court.

A FEDERAL JUDGE

In 2012, President Barack Obama **nominated** Ketanji to serve as a district court judge in Washington, D.C. A district court is a trial court for people accused of federal crimes. In 2013, Ketanji's nomination was confirmed, or accepted.

Ketanji continued in this role, or job, until 2021. That year, President Joe Biden nominated her to serve as a judge for the U.S. Court of Appeals in Washington, D.C. This is a higher court than a district court. It deals with appeals, or challenges to rulings by a lower court.

In Her Words

"I hope to inspire people to try to follow this path, because I love this country, because I love the law, because I think it is important that we all invest in [care about] our future … And the young people are the future."

— Answer during her Supreme Court confirmation hearings in March 2022

When a president nominates a person for a position as a federal judge, they must be confirmed by members of the U.S. Senate—part of the lawmaking body of the federal government. Ketanji has been confirmed multiple times with support from Senators with many different views. They've agreed she's a good choice!

A SUPREME CHOICE

In February 2022, President Biden announced that Ketanji was his choice to replace Stephen Breyer on the Supreme Court when he retired, or stepped down. Ketanji then had to go through confirmation hearings. During these hearings, U.S. Senators asked her questions about her rulings as a judge and her beliefs about the law to make sure she was the right person for the job.

The Senate confirmed Ketanji's appointment to the Supreme Court, and she joined the court on June 30. As the first Black woman to serve on the Supreme Court, Ketanji made history!

In Her Words

"It has taken 232 years and 115 prior [earlier] appointments for a Black woman to be selected to serve on the Supreme Court of the United States. But we've made it. We've made it, all of us. All of us."

— Speech given on April 8, 2022

Ketanji is shown here with President Joe Biden and Vice President Kamala Harris. Kamala and Ketanji are both groundbreaking women. In 2021, Kamala became the first woman—and first Black American—to serve as vice president.

A NEW POINT OF VIEW

Ketanji has brought a different perspective, or view, to the Supreme Court. She has worked as a public defender, which helped her better understand people accused of crimes. She also serves as a voice for Black women on the highest court in the United States—a place where they were never **represented** before.

Ketanji has used her voice to make a difference on the Supreme Court. In one example, Ketanji wrote what's called a dissent when she disagreed with the majority of the court's ruling on **affirmative action**. Ketanji's dissent helped people understand why Black Americans would be hurt by the ruling.

In Her Words

"Our country has never been colorblind."

— Dissenting opinion on *Students for Fair Admissions, Inc. (SFFA) v. President & Fellows of Harvard College (Harvard)* and *SFFA v. University of North Carolina (UNC)* from June 2023

The Life of Ketanji Brown Jackson

1970
Ketanji Brown is born on September 14 in Washington, D.C.

1988
Ketanji graduates from Miami Palmetto Senior High School in Florida and starts college at Harvard University in Massachusetts.

1992
Ketanji graduates from Harvard.

1996
Ketanji finishes studying at Harvard Law School and marries Patrick Graves Jackson.

2000
Ketanji's daughter Talia is born.

2003–2005
Ketanji works for the U.S. Sentencing Commission.

2004
Ketanji's daughter Leila is born.

2005–2007
Ketanji works as a federal public defender.

2010
Ketanji returns to the U.S. Sentencing Commission in a leadership position.

2012
President Barack Obama nominates Ketanji to serve as a district court judge.

2013
The U.S. Senate confirms Ketanji's nomination, and she begins working as a district court judge in Washington, D.C.

2021
Ketanji becomes a judge for the U.S. Court of Appeals in Washington, D.C.

2022
On June 30, Ketanji becomes the first Black woman to serve on the U.S. Supreme Court.

2023
Ketanji writes a powerful dissent after the Supreme Court rules to end affirmative action in colleges and universities.

Ketanji Brown Jackson has shown many young women, especially young Black women, that they can succeed in the fields of law and government.

AN INSPIRING STORY

Ketanji has come a long way from speech and debate competitions in Florida! However, she knew even then that her words mattered and that she could use them to make a difference.

Today, Ketanji makes a difference in many ways as a Supreme Court justice. One of the most important ways she makes a difference, though, is by being herself. Her story has inspired many people to believe they can do great things—and that they don't have to change anything about themselves to do them. That's a powerful way to make a difference!

In Her Words

"The notes that I've received from children are particularly cute and especially meaningful because, more than anything, they speak directly to the hope and promise of America … Our children are telling me that they see now, more than ever, that, here in America, anything is possible."

— Speech given on April 8, 2022

Be Like Ketanji Brown Jackson!

If two of your friends are arguing, listen respectfully to both sides before choosing who you agree with.

If you school offers it, sign up for the speech and debate team or the mock, or pretend, trial team.

Work hard in school, and be proud of your hard work.

Run for student government at your school.

Learn more about Black history and how racism affects Black Americans today.

Ask questions and learn more about how our government works.

Stand up for people who are being treated unfairly, and treat them with kindness.

Be brave enough to be yourself, even when you feel different from the people around you.

Write to government leaders about laws you feel are unfair.

Ketanji Brown Jackson's parents taught her from a young age that she could make a difference in the world. These are just some ways you can make a difference too!

GLOSSARY

accuse: To blame.

affect: To produce an effect on something.

affirmative action: The use of laws, rules, and other ways of doing things to improve opportunities in schools or workplaces for people from certain groups who've faced discrimination, or poor treatment because of something they cannot control.

competition: An event in which people try to win.

debate: An argument or discussion about an issue, generally between two sides. Also, to take part in such an argument or discussion.

dedicate: To commit to a goal or way of life.

federal: Relating to the central government of the United States.

generation: A group of people born during the same time.

guidance counselor: A person who gives help and advice to students.

inspire: To move someone to do something great.

nominate: To suggest someone for an honor.

represent: To act officially or stand for someone or something.

sentence: To give a formal judgment that states how a person who is found guilty of a crime is to be punished.

FOR MORE INFORMATION

WEBSITES

The Supreme Court of the United States: Justices

www.supremecourt.gov/about/justices.aspx

The official website of the U.S. Supreme Court offers facts about all the current justices, including Ketanji Brown Jackson.

What Are the Branches of Government?

bensguide.gpo.gov/a-what-are-branches

Ben's Guide to the U.S. Government offers this simple look at the three branches of the U.S. government, including the judicial branch.

BOOKS

Gaston, Stephanie. *Ketanji Brown Jackson.* New York, NY: Crabtree Publishing Company, 2023.

Hansen, Grace. *Ketanji Brown Jackson: US Supreme Court Justice.* Minneapolis, MN: Pop!, 2023.

Moses, Shelia P. *Who Is Ketanji Brown Jackson?* New York, NY: Penguin Workshop, 2022.

Publisher's note to educators and parents: Our editors have carefully reviewed these websites to ensure that they are suitable for students. Many websites change frequently, however, and we cannot guarantee that a site's future contents will continue to meet our high standards of quality and educational value. Be advised that students should be closely supervised whenever they access the internet.

INDEX